Antique collectors Guides

SWEETMEAT and JELLY GLASSES

by
Therle Hughes

Series Editor: Noël Riley

LUTTERWORTH PRESS
Guildford, Surrey

First published 1982

Cover illustration shows early Georgian dessert
glasses. *Left* a flared double-ogee bowl on teared
knop and domed foot, the bowl with
double-B handles, *c.* 1735. *Centre* a
diamond-moulded double-ogee bowl on inverted
baluster stem and radially moulded foot.
Ht. 5¼ in., *c.* 1740. *Right* a single-handled
syllabub glass with pan-topped bowl, knopped stem
and domed foot all finely reticulated, *c.* 1750.

ISBN 0 7188–2538–1

Printed in Great Britain by
Mackays of Chatham Ltd

Contents

Introduction

THIS book is intended to suggest the fascinating possibilities of collecting some of the finest glassware ever to gleam and sparkle on English tables, long overlooked by connoisseurs of drinking glasses. One of the pleasures of preparing such a book is the opportunity it offers to discover fellow enthusiasts with a shared admiration for past – and present – craftsmen and their superb lead crystal, world-renowned for centuries as flint-glass. I am extremely grateful to those who have given time and thought in helping me to select illustrations worthy of my subject. These include treasured pieces from fine private collections and notable specimens, too, from museums in glass-making regions of London, the West Midlands and the North where readers may go and see for themselves – and by looking learn far more than my words can ever convey.

1.   How They Were Used

FOR the freshest frothing syllabub our ancestors milked an obliging cow directly into a bowl of spiced and sweetened sherry or cider. They diced and candied citron peel into crisp little suckets dipped in hot barley-sugar with a silver spoon, but for strongly flavoured 'kissing comfits' to sweeten the breath they were prepared to coat each single caraway seed, say, or fragment of ginger or violet, with a sugary paste before jostling them over a charcoal fire – six separate coatings and cookings for aniseeds and as many as twelve for caraways, to make pea-sized cachous (figs. 1–5).

The sharp flavour of October quinces might be caught in a quiddany jellied with the juice of apple parings, but from at least as early as Stuart days Yorkshire Christmas fare included spiced orange jelly presented in cut quarters of the dried skins. And, as every good cook used to know, such jelly had to be prepared from long-boiled calves' or poultry feet or shavings of hart's horn or strips of un-

1–5. Stemmed glasses for finger-lifted sweetmeats – decorative work for the 18th century dessert (fig. 4 for comfits).

6. Fluted jelly glass, with heavy base and small domed foot.

reliable isinglass obtained from fish and clarified with egg-white, all strained repeatedly to show to advantage in flute-cut jelly glasses (fig. 6). Yet another kind of jelly required the starch of oatmeal or ground rice, spiced and sweetened to serve with wine and cream. This was the long-relished flummery, differentiated by country women from their frumenty, a jelly of fresh wheat with honey, eggs and sultanas (traditional doorstep peace-offering to fairies).

Ice cream, of course, had to be set in natural ice and salt (a process somewhat simplified for late Victorians by patented 'ice caves') by cooks who expected their underlings to spend long hours beating eggs by the dozen and cream by the pint for all their spicy wine-rich

7–9. Georgian custard glasses, fig. 8 with a domed base or 'kick', an early aid to annealing or toughening the glass.

custards (figs. 7–9). Half-an-hour's beating, for instance, was necessary even for the simple Naples biscuits described *In an Eighteenth Century Kitchen*, c.1716, by Dennis Rhodes and half-an-hour again for the cream and lemon and raisin wine of a 'solid' or 'whipped' syllabub, such as Maria Rundell declared would keep for as long as ten days (*Domestic Cookery for Private Families*, 1806).

Only when collectors realize the complexity of early sweetmeats and jellies can they appreciate the thinking behind the delightful little glasses here surveyed. It cannot be emphasized too strongly that dessert under whatever name was a decorative occasion enjoyed by the well-to-do and the glassware that furnished it had to be the finest and most newly fashioned (fig. 10).

Most conspicuous among dessert vessels are those that suggest clearly distinguishable variants of drinking glasses. There are, for example, the little 'dry sweetmeat' or sucket bowls on tall stems, the stemmed saucers or comports (fig. 11) and the stemmed plates or tazzas. All these would be for such finger-lifted sweets as flower candies, marshmallows, blanched almonds, 'chips' of orange and bergamot fruits and the strongly-flavoured comfits that required the tiniest vessels (fig. 12).

Thick sturdy glasses, tapering from rim to foot and with no more than the briefest of stems (figs. 13–15), have always been associated with jellies (filled hot) and ice creams (kept chilled) and here again collectors distinguish these from drinking glasses, such as short ales and drams.

Variants of the jelly glass may suggest the outline of a saucer above a cup and it is assumed that these offered whipped syllabub with its topping of curdled cream and doubtless other decoratively garnished goodies. But many a handsome stemmed glass, too, has this

10. The present century's meticulously exact cutting of curves and minute diamonds from lid finial to foot on a covered sweetmeat of the 1920s.

11. Small comport with fluted hollow stem, the bowl and foot showing rich diamond cutting.

12. Tiny tazza of about 1730, its top mould-shaped with a trellis pattern and its ribbed trumpet stand given extra strength with a folded edge.

pronounced double curve (fig. 16) and argument continues as to whether these costly vessels ever held champagne.

The rare, two-handled, spouted posset pot (fig. 85), may be seen as a forerunner of the shapely designs found among handled custard cups of the 18th and 19th centuries for all the veloutée creams and baked-egg trifles garnished with nutmeg or myrtle sprigs (fig. 17).

Added to such an array of little footed or stemmed-and-footed glasses must be the small ornamental plates for fruits and cheeses, wafers and the tiny feather-light meringues known as almond and chocolate puffs. Often these tasty mouthfuls were in themselves elaborately decorative, such as the *bouchées des dames* made from a paste of rice flour, eggs and sugar stamped into fancy shapes and colourfully glazed, as recommended by the early Victorian Scottish cook Mistress Margaret Dods of St Ronan's Spa.

There would be baskets and bowls too and, in contrast, the early Georgian massive glass salvers. Two or more of these wide glass plates on substantial stems could be arranged on top of each other in graduated sizes as the 18th century's greatly admired pyramid, each salver ringed with individual glasses of sweetmeats and jellies (fig. 18). This was rivalled only by the glittering glass épergne fashionable from the 1760s into Victorian days.

In later pages I trace the changing styles of all these delightful glasses but today's collectors can only enjoy them to the full when they can envisage how once they were presented. For many centuries magnificent feasting met men's need to celebrate success, to declare their status among rivals, to remember anniversaries and express the sheer joy of living

13–15. Handsome early glasses for 'wet sweetmeats' which collectors usually differentiate as for custard, jelly and syllabub respectively.

16. (*above*) Early 18th century glass with the double-ogee bowl shaping, sometimes considered to be for champagne.

among friends and family (fig. 19). Somewhat belatedly collectors of table glass are now recognizing how importantly sweetmeats graced such occasions. Eventually a collection may illustrate almost every decorative style associated with the more frequently collected drinking glasses and also show many details suited only to their own varied and appetising contents (fig. 20).

Early revellers required their food to be varied, their wine flowing freely. But we do our ancestors less than justice if we overlook the great care and skill that went into its presentation, especially in the entertainment long known as a fruit banquet, a term taken from the sideboard displaying light refresh-

17. Victorian custard cup with wheel-cut ornament in Stourbridge glass. Height 3½ in.

18. Glass salver with individual jelly and custard glasses.

ments in contrast to heavier foods eaten around a table.

Typically as early as 1591 the Worshipful Company of Drapers decided to change their annual festivities from a dinner to a banquet and by 1657 the Goldsmiths' Company could refer to a banquet of fruit 'according to the custom of the day'.

This insubstantial feasting with all the glitter of a fashionable social occasion was recalled by such diarists as John Evelyn who referred in 1682 to 'a great banquet of sweetmeats and music'. A ball reported by the *London Gazette* in 1703 'ended in a very handsome Banquet of Sweetmeats'. But to 18th century Georgians this kind of meal was usually called a dessert, often with a throng of guests standing and moving among the array of drinks and sweetmeats (fig. 21) as informally as at a 20th century cheese-and-wine party.

In a stately home such entertainment might be presented during the summer in a picturesque, airy 'banqueting house' commanding views over surrounding parkland. Even when the dessert immediately followed the dinner it was most handsomely laid out in a separate apartment: in 1800 Southey noted the drawing room as 'the common place for banqueting or of eating the dessert'.

Early instructions for the ornamental meal

19. Seventeenth century sweetmeat glass elaborately decorated in the style renowned as *façon de Venise*, the coiled stem enclosing a white thread and supporting pinched ornaments in blue.

20. Characteristic 18th century glass for rich custard and similar spoon-supped sweetmeats. With ribbed trumpet bowl and matching moulded knop.

21. (*below*) Magnificent sweetmeat glass of about 1725 with inverted baluster stem and deeply domed foot.

offer many clues to the collector seeking to identify the different uses of the sweetmeat glasses once arranged with such care by confectioners or by the professionally instructed daughters of wealthy families – an accomplishment long known as 'dressing out the dessert' (figs. 22–26).

Writers of the day were full of praise for such festivities. That invaluable recorder of thrifty good living, Lady Grizel Baillie, in her *Household Books*, 1692–1733, described parties of the 1720s offering glasses piled with French plums, apricots, almond biscuits and wafers on the lowest tier of a salver pyramid, with a second tier offering fruit jellies, lid-covered

22–26. Luxury sucket glasses with highly skilled cut ornament to sparkle in the party candlelight. Fig. 24 would be a top-glass, 7¼ in. tall.

sweetmeats and other tall glasses, all surmounted by a third, smallest salver offering white comfits around a central scalloprimmed top-glass: this would be a particularly fine version of the stemmed sucket glass, often more than seven inches tall (fig. 27).

A leading early Georgian professional cook, Mrs Hannah Glasse, suggested filling a three-tier pyramid 'with all kinds of wet and dry sweetmeats in glass, baskets or little plates, coloured jellies, creams, etc., biscuits, crisped almonds and little knick-knacks, and bottles of flowers prettily intermixed, and the little top salver must have a large preserved fruit'. It is difficult to imagine that such splendour escaped gigantic disasters: on one occasion in 1758 at a banquet attended by the Prince of Wales, Horace Walpole noted pyramids even on the chairs.

Dressing out the dessert involved the arrangement of all this glittering glass and colourful wines and sweetmeats on appropriately decorated tables: the Chelsea porcelain

27. Top-glass surrounded by jelly glasses on a stemmed salver, all richly engraved with matching ornament.

factory, for example, listed many of their delightful little glistening white figures as table ornaments 'for a desart'. But collectors concentrating on Victorian table glass are sometimes surprised to find how long the fashion persisted. At the Great Exhibition, 1851, sets of gilt-enriched dessert ornaments were offered in white parian porcelain, and Worcester in 1853 issued the celebrated Shakespeare dessert service illustrating *A*

28. Early 18th century glass, the bowl protected by gadrooning and the stem with an interesting incised surface twist, forerunner of air-twists.

29. (*below*) Quality features in a sweetmeat glass of about the 1730s include the deeply shaped double-ogee bowl with a cut arch-and-point rim and the domed and folded foot.

Midsummer Night's Dream.

Indeed the whole happy notion of the decorative dessert party has been unduly restricted by some collectors. In 1829 the wholesale price list of the Rotherham, Yorkshire, Glass Works included two qualities each of sweetmeats, syllabubs, jelly glasses and custard cups (fig. 32). They listed also ice cups, ice plates, baskets, top-glasses and salvers (as distinct from confectioners' glasses and covers).

Through Regency days a crowded informal social gathering might be known as a rout, and when, for the leisurely rich, even breakfast might be a party, the long night might end with a 'standing supper'. In the mid-19th century Mrs C. I. Johnstone described this as a bright, showy, exhilarating repast with flowers, colours and lights and with 'ornamental confectionery eaten on one's knees or standing'. At the same time under the term dessert she advocated 'creams, jellies and preserved fruits or compôtes' decoratively presented in 'richly cut and brightly washed *useful* articles of glass and china'.

Mrs A. B. Marshall, writing in the late 1890s, indicated the continuing demand for sweetmeat glasses in her list for 'a modern dessert' which included 'ices, sweetmeats of all sorts, fruits of all kinds, fresh and crystallized, biscuits both sweet and plain and last but not least, olives'. She noted that the sorbet was 'now assuming the importance of a special course in the dinner', having evolved from

30. Glass and silver epergne in the low, gracious style of the 1800s. Height 11 in.

31. (*left*) Characteristic covered sweetmeat dish of about 1810 with the deep mitre cutting that suited flint-glass 'fire'.   32. (*right*) Custard cup attractively moulded with wide facets and with a shapely little handle. Second quarter of the 19th century.   33. (*below*) Typical rounded bowl and slender stem in a pêche melba glass of about 1900, interestingly engraved with the willow pattern.

the popularity of spicy rum-and-lemon punch served semi-frozen. Prepared as an insubstantial lemon-water ice, flavoured with spirit and garnished with fruit, it was offered in individual cups and glasses and 'many pretty designs are specially made for this purpose'.

2.   How They Were Made

AN occasional rare sweetmeat glass remains to remind us of early Venetian splendour (fig. 34) with fantastic shaping of the fragile glass – fashionable throughout Europe as *façon de Venise* (enthusiastically revived in the 19th century). But early glass was too fragile for daily use. The great advance in the presentation of desserts came from the 1670s onwards with the development of England's brilliantly successful and long unrivalled flint-glass as it was always called, now more generally and logically known as lead crystal. Here the pioneer was George Ravenscroft, 1618–81, who produced a sturdy glass, heavy with lead, showing great refractive brilliance and a dark shadowy gleam within its depths and emitting a son-

34. Flamboyant Venetian work of the 16th century, the clear glass decorated with blue stripes.

35. (*above*) Slice cutting on the bowl of an early 18th century luxury sucket glass with a decorated knop-and-pedestal stem and domed foot.

orous ring when struck. Soon all the important suppliers of English table glass were using Ravenscroft's splendid flint-glass and a collection of 18th and 19th century sweetmeat vessels can show a remarkable range of their skills.

In 1745 a tax-by-weight on glass of a penny per pound of the materials – doubled in 1777 – prompted the development of lighter designs in keeping with current fashion, while improvements in furnace control to anneal or toughen the glass meant that vessels became increasingly amenable to the various delicate grinding wheels used by both glass engravers and glass cutters. Francis Buckley noted a German importer's advertisement for 'cut and carved dessert glasses' as early as 1709 and advertisements for such English work by the 1730s (fig. 35).

Many small solid details such as feet and pedestal stems might be shaped in hand moulds ('pinched') in the 18th century (fig.

36. Sweetmeat on square plinth with a central ridged hollow known as a lemon-squeezer foot.

36). But only from the 1830s and much more widely by the 1860s were the major hand processes more cheaply imitated by machine pressing. Until then every piece of hollow ware such as the bowl of a sweetmeat glass had to be formed by the glass-blower and his team or 'chair' by methods largely unchanged to this day.

Blowing down a hollow metal rod, he inflated a blob of hot glass gathered on its end from the melting pot, like treacle. In free-blown glass this bubble of glass had then to be manipulated into the required bowl shape, reheated as needed to keep it pliable and constantly twisted and turned to retain its symmetry while it was trimmed and shaped, completed with stem and foot and taken away to the annealing oven for toughening.

In blown-moulded glass the blob of hot glass was first blown into a mould to introduce the basic shape and surface pattern before further blowing and trimming as above.

37. Plain bowl on hollow stem with folded foot, free-blown about 1740.

38. Bowl on heavy knopped stem and lemon-squeezer foot. The cut lozenge ornament is often known as the Irish vesica pattern.

Full-size open-and-shut moulds for blown-moulded glass were mainly developed in the early 19th century but from about the 1830s shape and ornament might be achieved by mould-pressing without involving the glass-blower. This process was immensely important by the 1860s, producing ornament in clear-cut relief by forcing the hot glass into patterned moulds with a metal plunger.

Collectors date their sweetmeat and jelly glasses by looking closely and handling the lustrous old glass (fig. 37) as well as by observing the changing details of shape and ornament in bowl, stem and foot. They learn to recognize the faintest hint of dusky colour that varied in tone as glassmen tried to neutralize the impurities in their ingredients, aiming to produce the clear colourless 'white-ness' achieved by Victorian days.

Variations in tint are best observed by placing the glassware on white paper. On this point it may be mentioned that old tales about a recognizable colour in Irish glass have long lost credence. However, between 1780 and 1825 some distinctively massive table glass came from Ireland, free of taxes and other

39. Clear glass of about the 1740s in a range of sweetmeat shapes with matching wheel-engraved ornament.

restrictions (fig. 38). When the English tax was imposed in 1825 prosperity waned.

By turning and twisting a vessel the collector can look deeply into its substance, finger-tips appreciating its lustrous surface, considered worthy of expensive decoration such as individual hand-worked engraving (fig. 39) despite inevitable imperfections. Common flaws included swirling ripples inside the bowl, tiny bubbles and lines and the occasional specks that indicate imperfect fusing of the glass ingredients in the melting pot. Inferior glass advertised as tale metal came from top or bottom of the pot.

Often it is possible to feel a slight thickening around the rim where the bowl was sheared

40. Moulded shell sweetmeat in Silesian glass of about 1730, speckled with minute bubbles, the rim gilded, the stem and foot with slight cut ornament.

41. Slender 17th century glass with folded rim in fragile soda glass from the Netherlands.

from the blowing iron and even a trace of irregularity where this cut ended. There may be faint marks, too, where pincers, like giant sugar tongs, were used to maintain the shape of the bowl's hot, unstable glass.

Always of course there is the distinctive weightiness of English flint-glass, due to its lead content, when vessels are compared with those, often in similar shapes and known as *façon d'Angleterre*, in the Continent's most usual soda glass (figs. 40, 41). Late in the 19th century, for easier handling, the lead content might be reduced and today some glassmakers use 'lead glass' (with only 10% lead oxide content) or 'lead crystal' (25%) but they still keep to the original formula including 30% lead oxide for their loveliest 'British full lead crystal'.

At the same time collectors look for any concealed imperfections. Most obvious perhaps is the bowl or foot rim that has been trimmed to remove a chip and so lacks the rounded silky-smooth edge expected of old glass. Or there may be unconvincing scratchy 'wear marks' to the underside of a new foot. A fake may even show a hollow made under the foot to suggest removal of a (non-existent) pontil scar (*see below*). New, grey-looking wheel-engraving may have been added to an old bowl, not to be confused with the attractive needle-fine line patterns (fig. 42) etched on the glass with acid and popular from the later 19th century onwards.

The Victorians' mould-pressed ornament may sometimes be distinguished from free-hand deep cutting by the rounded base to each deep 'cut', in contrast to the sharp V-angles made by the glass-cutter's grinding wheels. However, even this could be rectified when the pressing was touched up on a cutting wheel. And a mould-shaped vessel could always be 'fire polished' – held in the heat of a small furnace to acquire a lustrous surface and

42. Pattern of very fine lines acid-etched on a custard glass from Stourbridge of the late 19th century. Height 3¼ in.

43. Duelling horsemen and other vivid details engraved on a Silesian glass of the 1730s–40s.

44. Slice cutting and arch-and-point rim harmonizing with cutting on the foot of a top-glass 7 in. tall, given extra height with beaded knops above and below the pedestal.

remove the raised thread-like lines left where the hot glass penetrated into the mould-joints.

Every collector quickly becomes familiar with the rough pontil or punty mark that recalls how the hot glass vessel had to be held by the base of the foot on a metal rod when its rim was cut from the blowing iron. The scar was made when the vessel was finally tapped free of the rod. It was soon minimized by smoothing on good quality glass and largely disappeared in early Victorian days when the foot was held on the end of the rod by a spring clip known as a gadget.

After slow annealing the free-blown glass vessel was ready for ornament. As befitted such luxury ware, some was gilded, for instance by James Giles, 1718–80, whose London workshops listed sweetmeats, syllabubs and jelly glasses in the 1770s. Other fine glass was engraved: this was developed especially on continental glass (fig. 43) which responded less brilliantly than flint-glass to cut ornament. Both engravers and cutters have always been specialist craftsmen using a wide range of tiny revolving wheels to grind their contrasting patterns into the surface of the glass. Engraving with a diamond point is rare and by diamond-cutting the glass collector usually implies wheel-ground V-shaped hollows (known as mitre-cuts) criss-crossing the glass to leave tiny points in sharp relief.

It is fascinating to observe how perfectly patterns were cut over the glass surface, for all of course were worked freehand, by holding the vessel up against the revolving wheels. (In contrast Victorian cutting might be based on mould-pressed shaping.) At first the glass surface was only shallowly ground away in simple geometrical patterns known as 'flat' or 'slice' cutting (fig. 44). From this developed facet-cutting which, like contemporary jewellery, was conceived to make the

45. Magnificent lidded sweetmeat glass, the richly cut ornament including facet-cutting on the lid finial and stem.

most of itself at later 18th century parties, routs and soirées held in the evening and lit by innumerable flickering candles (fig. 45). Small shallow hollows in long-diamond, hexagonal or scale shapes were cut contiguously so that the whole area of a vessel's stem and sometimes also bowl and foot – and often indeed the whole great spread of a glass épergne – sparkled and shimmered with a myriad tiny fires.

Regency and late Georgian (that is, pre-Victorian) fashion is associated with a pompous splendour that well suited the rich fire of British (and Irish) flint-glass, which was then flamboyantly cut in deep relief (fig. 46) with horizontal prisms, vertical ribs and flutes and wide areas of diamond points. Deep cutting has alternated with surface engraving ever since.

Less costly blown-moulded patterning has

46. Heavy cutting including the deeply waved edge known as vandyke shaping and a massive fluted stem on an Irish pineapple holder, c. 1790.

47 (*left*) Ornate little sweetmeat glass of about 1730, its fashionable double-ogee bowl mould-shaped with vertical flutes matched by the shaping of the highly domed foot and further enriched by the elaborate triple-collared stem with a flattened ball knop. 48, 49. (*right*) Effective dimpled patterning on mid-18th century sucket glasses with flute-moulded pedestal stems.

its own characteristics (fig. 47) and its gentle undulations can be felt by the fingertips both inside and outside the glass. The collector may observe a 'hammered' or dimpled surface (figs. 48, 49) or strengthening moulded ribs and note how the glassman has twisted these into a spiral, perhaps. Especially attractive is the smocked effect described at the time as nipped diamond-ways. In mould-pressing, in contrast, the metal plunger forced the glass vessel into the mould to give it a sharply detailed surface pattern with no corresponding undulations within it.

3. Stemmed Sucket Glasses and Stands

MOST collectors who concentrate on dessert glassware are attracted first by the elegant small-bowled stemmed and footed sucket glass, usually with a height of some five or six inches – even perhaps by this vessel at its tallest (as in fig. 44), sold as the pyramid's top-glass (still advertised in 1829). Many details such as bowl-rim and foot shaping and typical ornament may be noted too in the jelly, syllabub and custard glasses considered in later pages.

50. Sturdy sweetmeat glass showing the characteristic thick, everted rim, inverted baluster stem and small foot.

At first glance, stemmed sweetmeat glasses may resemble wine goblets but quickly reveal distinctive and most appealing differences. Characteristics include a bowl rim not only too thick-and-strong for a fashionable drinking glass but sometimes turned outwards (everted) or even fantastically decorated, a sturdy stem and, unlike the usual contemporary wine glass, a foot slightly smaller than the bowl-rim diameter. This meant that a single vessel could be lifted safely from a closely arranged group on the dessert table (fig. 50).

An early 18th century flint-glass vessel might continue earlier glass tradition by having a chip-defying folded-over rim. Bowl shapes included the outlines known as round-

51. (*above*) Fashionable double-ogee silhouette in the bowl of a 1740s sweetmeat glass moulded with vertical flutes to harmonize with the pedestal stem and domed foot. Height 5½ in.

52. Loops of glass attached to the bowl-rim with small glass prunts on a luxury glass of about the 1750s. With a white ribbon-twist stem and folded foot.

53. Wavy rim on a wide, shallow comfit glass with baluster stem and folded foot, precursor of many mid-Victorian frilled glasses.

funnel and ovoid and the most interesting double-ogee – an architectural term for a more or less pronounced S outline with the brief inward curve below the rim repeated in a curve perhaps halfway down the body of the bowl, giving a narrow section immediately above the stem (fig. 51). This is essentially a luxury shape and therefore to be expected on showy sucket glasses. It was most pronounced in what has come to be known as the pan-top syllabub glass.

The excitingly different feature of these 18th century sucket glasses, however, concerns their ornament, including features that surely suggest the glassman enjoying himself when not required to rim the bowl thinly for pleasant drinking. Most attractive decoration perhaps is a series of vertical arches or semi-circular loops of glass cut from rods and arranged round the rim, sometimes supporting a second tier and even a third, with small rosettes or prunts of glass to mask the joinings of loops and rim (fig. 52). Such an arcaded rim served to steady the highly domed and finialed

55. Luxury sweetmeat glass of about 1780 with fine cutting on rim, double-ogee bowl, cusped stem and domed octagonal foot. Height 6 in.

cover expected on many a now lidless sweetmeat (but not on all, to judge from records and trade-cards of their day).

A simpler alternative on some glasses towards the mid-18th century was the frilled or wavy rim (fig. 53), a variant being the 'dog tooth' pattern with a series of small squarish 'teeth' laid around a nearly flat rim (fig. 54). Both are to be noted on little comfit glasses. But the main early Georgian development in the bowls of stemmed sweetmeat glasses came from the specialist glass-cutter. Sweetmeat glasses were probably the earliest vessels to be so decorated in England and even by 1722 Lady Grizel Baillie was noting a high scalloped glass among an array of desserts: these were advertised through the 1730s. In 1727 she noted an advance in cutting technique, referring to a scalloped sweetmeat glass 'cornered brim'. The shallow slice cutting upon the surface of the glass was taken to its logical conclusion when the edge of the rim was cut to harmonize (fig. 55).

In considering their chronological history

the collector recognizes that sucket glasses shared characteristics with other stemmed and footed tableware in a sequence of styles through the 18th and 19th centuries, a period dominated by the fashioning of their stems. These may be summarized very roughly as: heavy balusters and inverted balusters, *c*. 1680s–1730s (fig. 56); moulded pedestal stems, *c*. 1710–1780 (e.g. in fig. 35); lighter inverted balusters and knops from the 1720s, popular again in the 19th century (figs. 57, 59–61); plain straight stems from about the 1730s onwards (fig. 58), enlivened with internal air-twist ornament from the 1740s, followed by opaque white enamel-twists from about 1755. These were outmoded from *c*. 1770

56. Early sweetmeat glass with folded rim and folded foot and an air-bubble 'tear' in the inverted baluster stem. Height 4⅜ in., *c*. 1700.

57–61. Sucket glasses and tazzas, the tallest 5¼ in., showing how the inverted baluster stem could be modified with knop shaping. Fig. 58 with straight stem.

by facet-cutting usually on hexagonal stems, straight or centrally knopped. Then came vertical fluting, followed by all the modifications of these outlines enjoyed by enterprising but history-revering Victorians.

The early sucket glass had a short massive stem, the then-fashionable baluster or rounded vase outline usually appearing as an inverted baluster with the greatest swelling close under the bowl. Lighter balusters were soon in fashion with early Georgians, however, along with more varied outlines such as a series of the solid swellings known as knops (fig. 62). Tiny bubbles of air pricked into the hot glass of such knops patterned them with 'beads'.

A particularly attractive alternative, adapted from silverware, was the pedestal stem (fig. 63) – strictly an inverted pedestal. This probably came to England from the Continent as early as Queen Anne's reign, although George I's arrival from Hanover in 1714 is sometimes suggested as the unlikely reason for its alternative name of silesian stem. Because of the sucket glass's luxury status this somewhat massive stem continued even into the 1780s. It was mould-shaped and tooled

62. (*above*) Small bowl, widely everted, on an unusual bobbin-knopped stem and domed foot. Height 5⅛ in. About the 1730s.

into a wide-shouldered tapering pillar, most usually eight-sided, semi-hollow or enclosing a 'tear' – perfect for grasping in a jostling crowd.

The sweetmeat foot, comparatively small as explained above, followed wine-glass outlines. Chipping was such a hazard in fragile continental glass that even in English flint-glass early fashion expected a folded-under foot rim, largely but by no means wholly abandoned after 1745. (Welted or folded feet were still advertised by late Georgian glassmakers.) The scratchy pontil scar necessitated a somewhat cone-shaped or prettier domed foot to keep it above the table top; more decorative feet included a central dome surrounded by a series of ridges ('terraced') or by a wide, nearly flat rim that is particularly attractive when dome and rim have been pinched into radiating ribs and bosses. In a facet-cut glass

63. Early Georgian glass with moulded stem, boldly ribbed for easy gripping and typically joined to the ribbed foot by a collar or triple merese.

64. Fine example of a double-series opaque white twist stem. The bowl shows lightly moulded writhen ribs. Height 5 in., c. 1760.

the domed foot might be faceted and scalloped to match (fig. 24).

Mid-18th century fashion enjoyed light-hearted rococo ornament, followed from the later 1760s onwards by a new and graceful interpretation of neo-classical symmetry. In fashion-conscious sweetmeat glasses of the 1740s–1770s the alternative to the pedestal was a straight slender stem charmingly decorated with an internal spiral. Early baluster stems had been enlivened with the long bubbles of air known as tears. But glass-men discovered that they could prepare long rods of glass filled with threads of air in increasingly complicated spirals and cork-

65. Lidded sweetmeat richly engraved on lid, bowl and foot, with air-beads in the knop finial and an air-twist stem enlivened with two knops.

screw twists encased within clear glass for cutting into stem lengths. These 'wormed glasses' were a clever English invention, some having white twists despite the extra cost of the enamel (fig. 64) and some with swelling knops to emphasize the pattern (fig. 65).

Many of the loveliest later 18th century sweetmeat vessels were mounted on stems and feet cut in the shimmering patterns known as facet-cutting. An especially attractive stem detail here was a central knop shaped in opposing curves, called a cusp. Around the end of the century and through Regency days this light-catching sparkle continued in stems cut with vertical flutes, known as bridge fluting when extended into the bowl. Cutting or moulded shaping on the foot included a ridged hollow under a handsome square plinth, known as a lemon-squeezer foot, followed by a round foot cut or moulded underneath with a star that became deeper and more elaborate by mid-Victorian days.

66. Later version of the lidded sweetmeat dating to around the end of the 18th century, with faceted lid finial, bold diamond and flute cutting and square lemon-squeezer plinth foot. Height 11½ in.

67. Deep mitre cutting on a mid-19th century custard cup in Stourbridge glass, including a broad star-cut foot. Height 4 in.

Short vertical flutes decorated many sweetmeat stems throughout the Victorian period and through much of the present century, becoming the basic outline for the workaday vessels eventually known to cooks merely as 'stems'.

Victorian sweetmeat glasses reflected the era's fondness for reviving 18th century fashions such as heavy arch-topped neo-Gothic fluting and the all-over patterns and spindly stems, including enamel twists, of 'revived rococo'. Some stumpy baluster stems in the mid-century 'Elizabethan' mood reflected the renewed interest in heavy mitre cutting that followed abolition of the glass tax in 1845 (fig. 67). There was even a mid-Victorian revival of early Venetian fantasies, applauded by such influential writers as Charles Eastlake in the 1860s.

Collectors soon recognize the Victorians' often imperfect understanding of earlier designs and proportions, as well as the extreme regularity and near-perfection of much of their

68. In contrast to fig. 67, this late 19th century Stourbridge custard cup is in clear ruby glass with a colourless glass handle and a plain flat foot. Height 3¼ in.

cutting, in conspicuously clear white glass.

As already explained, the foot by about the mid-19th century could be dully flat since it lacked any traces of a pontil scar (such as may be observed even on an early mould-pressed glass vessel when this was held on a rod in the heat of a small furnace or 'glory hole' for fire polishing).

By the 1860s the success of this mould-pressed glass in copying deep cutting, albeit clumsily, resulted in a change of high fashion towards greater use of colour (fig. 68) and much thinly blown glass decorated with engraving, which in turn prompted more inventive pressed designs. The conspicuous interest in engraved fern patterns in the 1860s–1880s has been traced to John Moore's *Ferns of Great Britain*, 1855. By then a widely favoured cheaper alternative to engraving consisted in patterning table glass with acid etching (fig. 42).

Ornament cut in deep relief soon returned to favour, however, and at the other extreme

69. Many-purpose 'stem' of about 1930 with radiant cutting on bowl, stem and foot.

the public's affection for miscellaneous small dishes, baskets and other bonbon vessels was met by the late Victorians' 'fancy glass'. Here it is enough perhaps to note that Harrods in 1895 observed a 'growing demand for Plain Table Glass'.

From such a survey it is interesting to observe the emergence of today's stemmed sweetmeat or sucket glass. Edwardian society still required small bowls for rinsing the fingers after dessert and sometimes a similar vessel was stemmed and footed to serve for either handed sweetmeats or spoon-supped delicacies. The old conventional styles of cut ornament continued to demonstrate their timeless appeal, including close vertical fluting such as the zigzags known as blazes, small lozenge-shaped groups of diamond-points and rows of the oval hollows known as printies or thumbprints.

An extremely interesting survey, 1925–1965, researched for me by Mr Tom Jones of

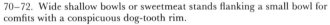

70–72. Wide shallow bowls or sweetmeat stands flanking a small bowl for comfits with a conspicuous dog-tooth rim.

73. Delightful little comfit dish only 2¼ in. tall in the Victorians' popular opalescent blue glass.

Royal Brierley Crystal, shows how the wide-based bowl has tended to become deeper and less expansive but has retained the sparkling cut ornament (fig. 69). Stems have been mainly slender balusters and inverted balusters with the occasional straight example centrally knopped, in contrast to the short heavy stems long associated with workaday pressed glass.

Many of the details that I have described for stemmed and footed sucket glasses may be noted at their most elaborate on the 'sweet-meat stands' included, for example, in a 1726 price list by Nat Barry of Bristol along with glass fruit baskets, jelly glasses and whip-syllabubs (figs. 70–72). Miniature versions, under four inches tall, might be given particularly conspicuous ornament to draw attention to their little piles of strongly flavoured 'hailstone' comfits. Porcelain figure comfit holders gesturing to their open bowls are now generally recognized for their one-time purpose in salon, parlour and hall but perhaps many a 'patch stand' or 'salt' should be associated with them too (fig. 73).

4. Comports

THE sweetmeat stand is particularly interesting in its Victorian manifestations as glassmen after 1845 showed off every kind of novel ornament – and the collector discovered just how enterprising they could be, especially in the important West Midlands glass-making area around Stourbridge and Dudley (now represented with great success in Broadfield House Museum of Glass, Kingswinford).

Dictionaries define a compôtier as a stemmed dish for a compôte of fruits in syrup and this presumably prompted the mid-Georgian adoption of the term comport (which became a compôte to genteel Victorians), used indiscriminately for any showy vessel with a tall stem supporting a wide shallow bowl for displaying the dessert's most elegant little finger-lifted delicacies. There are, for example, the heavily-cut massive designs often associated with untaxed Irish glass around 1800 (fig. 74); some have deep, rounded-over rims cut to harmonize with stems in the heavy ribbing called pillar fluting. But more imaginative decoration, with a hint of current interest in oriental and *art nouveau* design, is to be found in the deep engraving, polished to great brilliance, that recalls precious carvings in the translucent quartz known as rock crystal. This limpid rock crystal engraving of comports and other dessert ware was launched in the West Midlands in 1870 and continued until the mid-1920s.

Among comports especially the collector finds just how adventurous English glassmen could be when at last able to compete on equal terms with continental work in the use of colour. Here the collector may find the costly colour work known as casing, an ancient craft perfected in Bohemia and practised also in America. This used the marvellous ability of

74. Stars and swags below an ornate vandyke rim on a massively stemmed comport.

hot glass to fuse imperceptibly without inter-mingling. The bowl shape blown in glass of one colour was fitted inside one or more of other colours, all fused by heat. Patterns were ground into the resultant vessel down to a clear innermost layer, so that the slanting sides of the cuts would reveal lines of the intermediate colours.

5.   Jellies, Syllabubs and Custard Cups

75. Elaborate engraving
and facet cutting on a
Silesian gilt-rimmed
sweetmeat vessel of about
1750–60.

76. (*below*) Strong, firmly
based glass, blown-moulded
in a diamond trellis pattern
to high-light a colourful
jelly. Mid-18th century.

THE firm set of a jelly was a constant worry to 18th century cooks who welcomed the use of supportive individual glasses just as the hostess valued the colour and sparkle thus added to the dessert table. Some impressive continental work is found in the familiar jelly-glass form (fig. 75). But most of the vessels for jellies and custards confirm the supposition that they were the important workaday components of the 18th and 19th century dessert. For example, in 1746 the glassmakers Cookson, Jeffreys & Dixon of Newcastle-upon-Tyne, as noted by Francis Buckley, listed the components of a pyramid as four salvers, one top-glass, five top sweetmeats, but as many as thirty-two jellies and custards (total cost 42s. 6d.).

The typical jelly glass obviously made the most of this highly appreciated luxury, its narrow bell-shaped bowl still small of course, but with a total height of four or more inches to make a brave show on the pyramid (fig. 76). Some were cut and many blown-moulded in all-over diamond and rib patterns, coloured glass sometimes aiding the cook by further obscuring an imperfectly strained jelly (fig. 77).

Very many remaining jellies are plain but a valuable early example may have survived because it has a folded edge to the bowl's flared rim and the bowl set into a heavy, crack-defying gadrooned base. Flute cutting is particularly attractive and occasionally the bowl is vertically panel-moulded or is six-sided (figs. 78–83). A few show the horizontal ribbing known as Lynn rings. Scalloped rims were fashionable from the 1750s.

As well as a continuing abundance of blown-moulded jelly glass bowls, the 19th century offered opportunities for Victorian mould-pressed work of varying quality. Least

77. Fine ribbing given an attractive spiral twist in an 18th century blown-moulded jelly glass 4¾ in. tall.

78–83. An interesting range of jelly-glass treatment including cutting (figs. 78, 80, 82) and a rare six-sided vessel (fig. 79).

welcome to collectors are the glasses with plain conical bowls on thick disc feet, cheaply made for serving ice creams and the like in confectioners' shops. In contrast some good quality jelly glasses reflected the liking for tall attenuated vessels around 1900, being shaped like deep goblets on the period's very thin stems and flat feet. Some show an undulating surface, some cut or etched ornament.

Deep bowled glasses for whipped syllabub, on short knop stems – 'buttons' – or stemless, were listed separately from jelly glasses. Collectors distinguish them by their generally greater capacity and pronounced ogee or pan-top bowl shaping intended to support the rich frothy topping (fig. 84). For the ancient syllabub drink an obliging milkmaid, pasturing cattle in fashion-frequented parkland, might please a passing customer by milking a cow into a pan of sweetened ale or cider. The great George Ravenscroft took orders for lidded

84. Whipped-syllabub glass of about 1740 showing a merese beaded with air bubbles above the domed foot.

85. Two-handled posset pot, 3¼ in. tall, its narrow spout bearing the glass seal of George Ravenscroft's own glasshouse. Probably made for the Earl of Stafford who died 1695.

86. Magnificent set of syllabub glasses surrounding a tall-stemmed top-glass, on a salver that revolves upon its base, all richly cut.

syllabub vessels and collectors assume that these were the two-handled cups now generally called posset pots. Their unusual feature was the spout emerging from near the base, to ensure that the drinker enjoyed the rich liquor beneath the surface froth (fig. 85).

By early Georgian days, however, cooks were deliberately whipping their cream and adding lemon juice to the ale or wine to ensure a thickly curdled 'wet sweetmeat' instead of a drink. Mrs Glasse for example recommended that the whipped-up froth should be spooned off and laid gently over clear strained sack or claret. This concoction obviously was best served in the wide-topped vessel now associated with the cheerful name syllabub (derived, according to Bailey's early 18th century dictionary, from swilling bubbles).

The best whipped-syllabub glasses were wheel-cut on bowl-rim, body and foot to harmonize with the stemmed sucket glasses (fig. 86); many were vertically ribbed. But eventually syllabub glasses were forgotten, whereas in the late 19th century the vessels specifically named for ices, custards and jellies were constantly offered *en suite* with the rest of the table glass.

Custard cups with handles were popular throughout the 19th century and still widely used early this century. An early flat-based cup-shape for setting the egg custard in a pan of hot water continued into this century as an alternative to footed designs. But the 18th century's most charming vessel was the deep narrow bowl on an arching foot, graced with one or two handles shaped according to the glassman's whim with delightful little

87. Simple but shapely and unflawed fluted custard cup which would make an excellent start to a sweetmeat glass collection.

88, 89. Fluted custard cups that show the long-continued style of shapely up-curled handle.

flourishes. An urn-shaped cup on a pedestal foot suited the late 18th century's neo-classical mood and this style persisted through late Georgian and Victorian days. Handles, it appears, were always an optional extra. The single-handled, heavily fluted cup, sometimes tulip shaped, served the early Victorian, some vessels with knop stems having been noted in the 1850s. Small straight stems followed late in the century when often only the handle distinguished custard from jelly glass.

In order to avoid confusion these handles are worth consideration. Some substantial custard cups, like mid-Victorian and later jugs, have massive handles, broadly attached at the base and often tapering slightly to the shoulder (fig. 87). But the 18th century style of handle was so attractive – and so adequate for light-weight sweetmeats – that it is as often found on Victorian and later custard vessels. In this the narrow rod of hot glass was affixed first at the shoulder and curved downwards, ending in an elegant little curl (figs. 88, 89).

6. Dessert Table Salvers and Epergnes

90. Sturdy salver of about 1740 with a welted edge to its gallery rim, a hollow flute-moulded stem and a folded foot.

THIS survey would be incomplete without reference to the glass salvers carried by servants among party guests and making a splendid show when placed on top of each other to form the pyramid described on page 54 (fig. 90). The strong flint-glass evolved by Ravenscroft could bear a considerable weight and two-tier pyramids were in use by about the 1680s, the flat plate – still with the folded rim associated with more brittle soda glass – resting on a hollow bell-shaped pedestal.

As glass became stronger because better annealed the pyramids could be piled higher and also made more decorative (fig. 91). For close arrangement of the individual sweetmeat glasses they soon acquired low rims: some advertised as new-fashioned in the early 1760s had scalloped ornament on the rims of both plate and foot. The undersurface of the plate offered obvious opportunities for decoration, whether cut, engraved or mould-pressed with shallow geometrical patterns.

The moulded pedestal made a convenient stem but by the 1780s the lowest salver might have a massive spool-shaped support, immensely strong to bear the weight of the loaded pyramid. Illustrators of the 18th century's tradesmen's advertising cards made a magnificent show with cut-glass dessert pyramids.

A variant was a bottom salver made with a circular plate revolving on a gilded silver pivot fitted into the massive pedestal foot. Another was the sweetmeat stand with a series of glass plates in diminishing sizes centrally holed to fit over a tapering stem. This stem might be of glass but more enduringly was a hollow funnel of silver weighted with a heavy filling. But the main innovation from about 1760 was the glass epergne, inspired by the table candelabrum.

The epergne (from *epargner*, to economize) became fashionable in silver in about the 1730s, to present pickles and condiments on the crowded dinner table. Its central pillar on a wide foot supported not only a top dish but an array of out-curving arms each ending in a small vessel. Lady Grizel Baillie in the 1720s, as a guest of Sir Robert Walpole, observed one appearing on the table at every meal and I can imagine that many a hostess must have made the most of such a treasure by removing the little glass pickle and salt dishes and filling their perforated silver holders with colourful sweetmeats.

When the whole epergne was created in glass it was indeed a splendid spectacle with its central top bowl piled with fruit or suckets

91. Salver with a decoratively knopped stem, probably intended as the uppermost tier of a pyramid.

92. Early cream epergne entirely of glass, 9 in. tall, holding six hanging dishes.

93. The glass epergne at its most handsome with facet cutting on stem, scrolls and pendant drops, the urn-shaped body resting on a square plinth foot. Flanked by a pair of decanters.

and the branches holding dishes or hung with little glass baskets. This dated mainly from the 1760s onwards, eventually being taken over by late Victorians for elaborate flower arrangements. An early low style known as a cream épergne (fig. 92) had the central stem encircled with thick short hooks, bearing little glass pails for variously flavoured creams. But by the 1770s–1790s the glass epergne might be as much as eighteen inches tall.

The Mirror, no. 34, 1779, noted as a table centrepiece 'a sumptuous glass epergne filled with sweetmeats'. In this the central shaft would be topped by a richly ornamented dish and would support curved outspreading branches known as scrolls for smaller dishes or baskets, all scintillating with the period's facet-cutting and eventually further enhanced with festoons of cut-glass lustres or drops (fig. 93). Even the central shaft might be an elaborate composite stem, including perhaps an urn or pineapple motif.

From about 1780, however, the branches might be attached to the shaft by fitting into lugs of silver or double-gilded brass. The sweetmeat vessels too might be given basket handles of silver wire (fig. 94) and eventually the branches themselves might be of silver, ending in circular loops for little cut glass bowls (fig. 30).

Early Victorians with their love of naturalistic ornament might support lavishly cut bowls on extravagant silver work (fig. 95). But the term epergne might still be applied to a pretentious variant which could be wholly of glass (often introducing colour) because here too the purpose was mainly ornamental, with a single bowl for sweetmeats on an ornate supportive stem, introducing, for example, the

94. Glass epergne 17½ in. tall with scalloped top bowl and domed foot, its waved scrolls (sometimes called snakes) fitting silver lugs around the faceted glass stem and its twelve dishes hung on silver wires.

95. Extravagantly cut glass
on a silver epergne bearing
an inscription dated 1838.
The small dishes can be
replaced by glass candle
holders.

mid-Victorians' favourite close ribbing, trail-
ing and a peppering of small hemispherical
drops or beads. This was most popular in the
1860s–1870s and was more generally known
as a bonbon stand, a fruit-and-flower holder
or merely a centrepiece. It is recorded that
the West Midlands Richardson firm made a
three-tier glass centrepiece with twenty-eight
hanging baskets.

7.   Fancy Glass

COLLECTORS of glass sweetmeat vessels may find the epergne's little bowls, dishes and baskets in sparkling cut glass among the many others welcomed by late Georgians and Victorians as bonbon holders. Some rich blue glass is associated with the late 18th and early 19th centuries (fig. 96) but lighter, brighter colours (fig. 97) and opalescent effects (fig. 98) are found in abundance among the Victorians' 'fancy glass' – wavy edged, lacy, quilted, satin-surfaced, marble, ivory, the imitative effects applied to a vast assortment of equally imitative shapes, from art nouveau flowers (fig. 99) to cupped hands. Collectors today are often particularly attracted by early press-shaped plates, with crisp relief ornament applied to both surfaces, sometimes textured to suggest lace. The pressed cup-plate, three or four inches across, is not always identified for its original purpose – more American than British – of holding a china teacup while the

96. Engraved souvenir bowl in deep blue glass, 3¼ in. tall, its once-gilded ornament named as Yarmouth Bridge and hence attributed to the decorator William Absolon, at work in Yarmouth from the 1780s to 1815.

97. Stourbridge sweetmeat bowl 4 in. tall in ruby glass, its stem and foot in clear crystal to avoid the problem of exact colour matching. Victorian.

hot tea was sipped from the cup's saucer. Clever colour effects under many fancy names were most popular around 1870–1890 and in *English Nineteenth Century Press-Moulded Glass* C. R. Lattimore explains how to read the makers' symbols and diamond-shaped design registration marks.

Many items of fancy glass were intended merely as parlour ornaments but are pleasant little sweetmeat receptacles nonetheless. Some, superbly cut, date to the present century (fig. 100). Indeed a vessel's original purpose is often imprecise. Catalogues may illustrate the same bowls as finger glasses and, with loop handles, as bonbon dishes.

Misleading items worth bearing in mind include individual wineglass coolers, open-flame lamps, posy baskets, mignonette troughs, glass linings for silver condiment pots and urns and the handsome salt cellars that followed abolition of the salt tax in 1825. Among the most numerous are the glass sugar basins, covered and uncovered, copiously illustrated in Victorian trade journals. Pardonably, perhaps, even these may contribute beguilingly to the variety of small vessels when we dress out our desserts today.

98. Late Victorian Stourbridge dish in shaded pink opalescent glass with a green glass handle and shell feet.

8.   Prices

IN the early 1930s a purchaser of custard powder might obtain a stemmed sweetmeat glass as a free gift. I have some still. Bowl and foot were mould-patterned in semblance of simple cutting and linked by a short thick stem, all revealing to eye and finger the raised thread-lines left by the three joints in the mould. The glass itself is now somewhat grey and dull surfaced, but they have proved strong enough to weather fifty years of non-stop use, unchipped and saleable today at the bottom end of a market that appeals to many a collector by the range of prices among items still readily available up and down the country.

In the past, even 18th century sweetmeat glasses have tended to be overlooked by

99. Lively design probably intended as a combined bonbon and flower holder, a popular Victorian notion. In ruby and purple opalescent glass. Stourbridge, late 19th century.

100. Perfect conclusion to the fine craftsmanship illustrated throughout this book, a trefoil bonbon dish of the 1930s, the deep cross-cut diamond pattern contrasting with the fine irregular star cut into the base.

collectors intent on acquiring drinking vessels, and hence were underpriced. Victorian vessels were completely despised. Now however a new appreciation of their one-time luxury status has meant an increasing demand for those of fine workmanship and early date. The very fact that they were made with comparatively thick rims and small feet has meant that early specimens have survived in perfect condition, occasionally even from around the end of the 17th century – for example with a gadroon-protected folded-rim bowl on a heavy stem and folded foot. In the past year or two such a vessel has commanded a price of £100–£150. But an elegant early Georgian vessel, even with all the signs of original costliness such as a slice-cut double-ogee bowl, pedestal stem and ornate domed foot, may sell at less than half such a figure.

Some collectors are attracted especially by jelly glasses and custard cups and even today a specimen has to be very attractive to sell for over £50. As always it is the collector accustomed to the look and feel of old glass and high quality craftsmanship who may find bargains among the numbers still available in the £5–£10 range. A clear coloured glass such as a custard cup on an uncoloured stem and foot may be rather more costly so long as collectors favour even the most cheaply produced cranberry colour. Mould-pressed dessert plates and bonbon vessels in coloured opaque glass still sell for a few pounds too, with marbled colours more costly than the most familiar plain light blue. But collectors must be cautious when considering their major selling feature, the marks of maker and design registration sometimes included in the moulded ornamentation. The diamond-shaped registration mark can be interpreted to provide a date but not the date of the individual vessel: it indicates merely the launching of what may well have proved to be a design of very long or revived popularity.

Books for Further Reading

L. M. Bickerton *Illustrated Guide to 18th Century Drinking Glasses*
Francis Buckley *Old English Glass*
Derek Davis *English and Irish Antique Glass*
E. Barrington Haynes *Glass*
G. Bernard Hughes *English Glass for the Collector*
Therle Hughes *Small Decorative Antiques*
C. R. Lattimore *English 19th Century Press-Moulded Glass*
R. Wilkinson *The Hallmarks of Antique Glass*

Acknowledgements

The author and publishers would like to thank the following for permission to use the photographs in this book: Messrs Asprey & Co. 16, 21, 35, 45, 46, 54, 63; Messrs Bracher & Sydenham 95; Broadfield House Museum of Glass, Kingswinford 17, 42, 67, 68, 73, 97–9; Messrs. W. G. T. Burne Ltd 22–6, 30, 57–61, 86, 92–4; Messrs Christie's 52; Messrs Delomosne & Son *Front cover*, 1–5, 48, 49, 65, 70–2, 74, 91; A. Henning 13–15, 78–83; Honeyborne Royal Brierley Museum 10–12, 31, 33, 47, 51, 55, 66, 69, 76, 84, 90, 100; Mrs H. Hopley 99; Laing Art Gallery, Newcastle 27; Pilkington Glass Museum, St Helens 41, 85, 96; Messrs Sotheby's 40, 43, 62, 64, 75; Victoria & Albert Museum – *Crown Copyright* 20, 32, 34, 37, 39, 53, 56, 77; remaining items are taken from private collections.

Index

Bold numbers refer to illustrations